IT'S TIME TO GROW UP

Rooted And Grounded In Love

By Ricky Perrodin

INTRODUCTION

This is a book not written to impress you with big fancy words, Greek and Hebrew texts, and deep spiritual truths. I ask God to show me natural things, so that I can understand spiritual truths. Jesus used this method of teaching. He used things that were common to their everyday lives; things they worked with and understood. I will attempt to do the same thing in this book using an analogy of the Christian life and a tree planted in dirt. My hope and prayer is that God will use this simple teaching to minister to you as Jesus ministered to the people He lived with. Read the book. You can go back later and translate all the words you want to Greek and Hebrew. If the book does not apply to you today, keep it, tomorrow it probably will!

ANOTHER GREAT OPPORTUNITY TO TRANSPLANT

Everything was just going along fine…and then it happened. My wife, Sandra, comes home from work and says she was offered a job that was in another state. This job would probably mean twice the pay, twice the benefits, and twice the prestige. My immediate answer, "We're not moving, so forget it." Sandra agreed, but continued to give other details. "We are not moving!" I calmly but firmly replied. However, for the next couple of days I pondered the offer. Sandra and I discussed it several times. After all, we are believing to get out of debt. This would definitely help. I started questioning my quick "We're not moving!" answer. What if this was God? What if this was His way for us to get out of debt? Finally after praying about it for several days we were undecided and confused. We decided to ask our pastor to pray with us concerning the move. His response to our request caught me off guard. He said, "There is nothing for me to pray about, you are not going anywhere!" He didn't sugar coat it. He gave us the blunt answer that we needed to jolt us back to our original position; we are not moving.

Over the next several weeks I started thinking about where we were and how we got to this point in our lives. I thought about the move up to Northwest Arkansas and applying for elementary physical education teaching jobs. I discovered the Fayetteville and Springdale school districts at that time did not hire certified elementary P.E. teachers. So the circle broadened to include Farmington, Elkins, Rogers, Bentonville, Lincoln, and many others. Finally I had an interview with Decatur School District. Coming out of the interview with the elementary principal I told my wife, "I'll never work for him, he's a jerk!" Well, that was the only job I was offered, so I took it. Decatur is 39 miles and a 45 minute drive (each way) from where we were living. My thought was, once I get a job in Arkansas teaching, I can work my way back through Bentonville & Rogers to get a job closer. For several years I applied for positions. I was in the top two candidates once, but the other guy was chosen. To make matters worse Decatur paid about $5,000 less per year than the other districts. At the time of this writing the gap has widened to over $12,000 less per year than Bentonville/Rogers.

Continuing to look back where we came from, I thought of the principal I did not want to work for. He turned out to have a leadership style that allowed me to bloom as a P.E. teacher. As I bloomed, so did the P.E. program. This is by far the best program I have had in all my years of teaching. I have stopped looking at other districts for jobs, even though the pay is better. If those districts came to me right now and offered me a job, I would turn them down. The great program that some of them wanted in their school, and didn't think I could give them, I have in Decatur. As a matter of fact, a picture of our end of the year "Field Day" was on the front page of the Bentonville local newspaper! Even if they want me now, they can't have me, Decatur has me. You see, I'm planted.

Finally in all the thinking about what was happening in our lives, these scriptures came to be very meaningful: Ephesians 3:14-21.

"For this reason I kneel before the Father, from whom His whole family in heaven and on earth derives its name. I pray that out of His glorious riches He may strengthen you with power through His Spirit in your inner being, so that Christ may dwell in your hearts through faith. And I pray that you, BEING ROOTED AND ESTABLISHED IN LOVE, may have power, together with all the saints, to grasp how wide and long and high and deep is the love of Christ, and to know this love that surpasses knowledge- that you may be filled to the measure of all the fullness of God. Now to Him who is able to do immeasurably more than all we ask or imagine, according to His power that is at work within us, to Him be glory in the church and in Christ Jesus throughout all generations, for ever and ever! Amen."

There are a lot of things that we want in those verses: riches of His glory; strengthened with might; Christ dwelling in your hearts; comprehending and knowing the love of God; filled with fullness of God; do exceeding abundantly above what we ask. But the key to all this is in verse 17b "…being rooted and grounded in love." I saw where you have to be rooted and grounded to grow. My P.E. program is what it is today because I stayed in Decatur. I

<u>grew</u> because I stayed. The <u>program grew</u> because <u>I grew</u>. It was not always easy. The first two years the older elementary kids were brutal with me. When they didn't like the game we were playing, they would say, "we don't like you," "you're not a good teacher," "we want Mrs. Howard back." For two years plus that went on. I drove a school bus for a couple of years. I had some kids on that bus …. well let's just say I had to write referrals on them. The parents

would be upset when their child was kicked off the bus. Eventually some of the parents signed a petition and talked to the school board and the superintendent and tried to get me fired. So don't get the idea when I talk about what a good program I have NOW, that there weren't hard times along the way. You will have hard times if you decide to stay. You'll have hard times wherever you are! As one preacher use to say "I try to be positive in my preaching… And I am

Positive that you will have hard times." But I made it through those hard times. I have been there so long now, going into my twentieth year at this time in the writing of this book, that I am the only P.E. teacher the students have known in the elementary. I am planted, and I am reaping the benefits of staying planted in one place.

CAN'T WE JUST BE FREE FOR THE LORD TO USE?

Over the last 6 months the Lord has been dealing with me on the importance of having roots and being planted. He has given me several things in the natural to understand the spiritual principle. One of these examples is an artificial tree that was used on the platform in our church sanctuary. A couple of months ago the artificial trees were given new pots to give the stage a new look. I had not thought of it before this time, but have come to realize that under the pretty moss topping, these trees were held upright by Styrofoam and a wood board nailed to the bottom of the tree stump. After "transplanting" these trees to their new pots and restuffing them, one of them had a hard time staying upright. Then it dawned on me-this tree does not stand up right like a regular tree because it has NO

ROOTS! Since it has no roots, it is _not_ alive or growing. It is an artificial tree; it is a FAKE TREE! But it looks so good; it has been around for at least the 5 years we have been attending. But it hasn't grown a bit, and it has produced nothing-no flowers, no fruit, no nothing. The Lord told me that is how a lot of people are in the church. They look good, they may even attend regular for years, but if you don't have roots planted in love, you are dead, artificial, fakes. They will not grow. They will not produce any fruit.

The next illustration the Lord showed me had to do with my bonsai trees. I am working with some Mimosa trees. I started three trees in a pot almost a year ago now. One of the trees was about 4" tall, another 3" tall and the last 2" tall. The 4" tree is now about 14" tall (Daddy tree), the 3" tree is about 6" tall now (Mommy tree), and the 2" tree is still about 2" tall (the Baby tree).

About once a year you are suppose to clip the tree tops and roots. This helps them to be fuller on top and to dwarf the growth. The Lord showed me several things concerning these trees. One thing He pointed out is that these trees have real roots in real soil and are producing real branches. However, they are planted in the wrong place! You see there are some other trees that are growing outside in the same place that I dug these up from. The outside trees have grown about 4-5' in the same period of time. This year the outside trees even flowered. My Bonsai trees have never flowered. The difference between the trees is where the trees are planted. So an important point to be made is that we need to be planted in the right place-church, job, and friends, just to name a few. If you are in the wrong place, you will never reach your potential. You will not become all that God would have you to become. As a matter of fact, you will be a square peg in a round hole. You will also be messing up someone else's life. You will be filling the gap where they belong. Not only will you be miserable, but you will make everyone around you miserable. Look at the story of Jonah. Jonah, running away from God, endangered the lives of everyone on ship with him. The sad thing about the 3 trees I have planted is that the "Daddy" is experiencing some growth, maybe even enough to satisfy himself. But look at the growth of "Mommy tree". It is definitely experiencing only some of its potential. Poor "Baby tree" suffers the most. It has experienced almost no growth in a year's time. This shows the importance of good leadership by the mom and dad being planted in the proper place to promote growth in the kids. Very often it is the kids that suffer for the mistakes of Mom and Dad.

Another thing I learned by pruning the top 3-4" off the Daddy tree is, I'm taking the future away from this tree. At the very top is a new leaf unfolding, it will be the next branch at the top of "Daddy tree." However, when I trim the top of this tree (basically I give it a flat top) I take away its next leaf, the next branch. I am cutting off the entire future of where this tree was going. If this tree has the root system established like I think it does, this tree will not die, it will live. It will eventually produce not one, but several shoots out of the top to make new leaves and branches. Since this book is taking several months to get put together and I have the luxury of a computer, I can report to you that the daddy and mommy trees are beautiful just a month after its pruning. The baby tree died. What makes the difference is the root system. Have you felt that your entire future was taken from you-maybe the death of a mother/father, spouse, son/daughter, you lost your job, business, went bankrupt, lost your reputation/your good name? We had a swarm of bees land in our 15' oak tree. A bee keeper was called to remove the bees. After hours of work, he finally decided he would have to trim branches to get to the swarm. That did not work. He asked if he could cut the whole tree down. I asked if he would just cut it below the bees (about 6' up in tree.) He topped it off. Sure enough that spring and summer it grew five shoots, one becoming the main trunk. The oak had a good root system that over came the major set back.

What will make the difference for you is being rooted and grounded in love. You have to realize that this is a pruning, a minor set back (You have to change how you look at the circumstances of life from "my future has been cut off, I'm ruined" to "this pruning, this minor set back, will not last forever"). God has a future and a hope for you. "For I know the plans I have for you, declares the Lord, plans to prosper you and not to harm you, plans to give you hope and a future." Jeremiah 29:11. Some of the things that happen to you may be the devil, right straight from the pit of hell. "The thief comes only to steal and kill and destroy." John 10:10a. Some things that happen to you are from God. "He, (God), cuts off every branch in me that bears no fruit, while every branch that does bear fruit He prunes so that it will be even more fruitful." John 15:2. I won't take the time to figure out which one is happening in your life. That can be another whole book, and actually needs to be considered on a case by case basis. If there is any forgiveness or repenting to be done, take care of it. What I want you to know from this book is where you go from here. The first thing that comes to mind is you don't want to spend a lot of time "crying over the spilt milk." What has happened-happened! Now what? Well, what is going to happen depends on your root system. You see, my bonsai mimosa tree and the oak tree had a good root system, planted in good fertile soil that gets good light and all the fresh water it can drink. You know what is going to happen to my "flat top tree?" It not only is going to live and not die, but it is going to do better than it was before the clipping. You see the good root system is going to keep sending up all the building blocks it has been sending for growth. When it can't find its normal path, it is going to produce not one, but several new shoots. The end is better than the beginning.

Let's get back to you. You've just been clipped, pruned, a minor set back- (come on now, start getting this…A MINOR SET BACK!) It's time to do some growing. Jesus' disciples used to try to figure these situations out too. Actually in this story they have already jumped to the conclusion that sin is involved, they just want to know who did it. Jesus teaches them that His agenda is totally different.

"As Jesus passed by, He saw a man which was blind from his birth. And His disciples asked Him saying, Master, who did sin, this man, or his parents, that he was born blind? Jesus answered,

neither hath this man sinned, nor his parents: but that the works of God should be manifest in him."
John 9:1-3.

What I see from these scriptures is that no matter what, God wants you well. He wants to bring healing and restoration and new abundant growth in your life. God wants to manifest His love and goodness in your life. He wants you not just like you were before your "minor set back," he wants you better than you were before. New and improved, stronger and more fruitful than you ever thought was possible. You might have been "good" before, but now you are going to be "Better." You may have been at the "better" stage, but God wants to take you to the "Best" stage. You may have been at the "best you had ever been level," but God wants to take you to the level where you are rooted and grounded in His love! When you are rooted and grounded in His love, you know what's going to happen? The nutrients you get from His soil will produce branches, leaves, and fruit made in His image. You will be without spot or wrinkle and a bride worthy of His Son. That is what this world is looking for: Some people that know what it is like to "go through some stuff." But more than that, because a lot of people have gone through a lot of stuff just to come out on the other side bitter, hateful, calloused, hard hearted, and hard headed!

What the world needs is some people to come out on the other side full of love and compassion, that have experienced that hurt and pain that the world is in. The world needs people that will not judge them, as far as condemning them, but accept them where they are and love them into a restoration relationship with Jesus Christ.

GROW UP

The two pine trees outside the front door of our church serve as good examples of being rooted and grounded. They aren't easily moved: Criticism by other trees- "you got needles instead of leaves" just doesn't seem to affect them. They don't seem to even mind the name calling- "you are a sappy tree." They are not easily swayed by the ever changing winds.

"Then we will no longer be infants, tossed back and forth by the waves, and blown here and there by every wind of teaching and by the cunning and craftiness of men in their deceitful scheming. Instead, speaking the truth in love, we will in all things GROW UP into Him who is the Head, that is, Christ. From Him the whole body, joined and held together by every supporting ligament, GROWS AND BUILDS ITSELF UP IN LOVE, as each part does its work." Ephesians 4:14-16.

People today are looking for grounded rooted people. They are looking for solid, stable people. I once taught a kindergarten student that would cry every morning. I asked one person at school what the reason was. They said they didn't know, but if he was their kid, they would give him a good spanking and make him go to class. I asked someone else. They said the kid cries when his mother leaves his father. Whenever she would find a boyfriend she would leave the husband and the kids and live with the boyfriend till she was kicked out. Sometimes she would bring the boyfriends home. What a nice family environment that must have been. I realized the kid was just trying to cope with a lousy family life. I think I would cry too if I was in that situation. What the student needed was to be surrounded by people rooted and grounded in love. He needed stability in his life. We can't make these parents live right but we can help this kid walk through this period in his life knowing the love of Jesus and provide some stability to his life.

There are people all around us that are looking for the same thing this child was looking for. They are looking for some

Stable People. They are looking for people with not only their "heads screwed on straight', but 'screwed on to the right bolt'! We need to be screwed on in the right place. To keep the analogy- we need to be planted at the right spot. People, like this little child, need to be able to wake up in the morning and know that you are going to be there for them. To know you haven't switched jobs, apartments, cities, or states just to make a good career move. Many times they may never need you. They may not call you for counseling; they may not run to you with every problem. The security for them is JUST KNOWING YOU ARE THERE FOR THEM! That is where you being rooted and grounded in love comes in. It's time for some Christians to GROW-UP and accept the responsibility of being spiritual parents to a world filled with thumb sucking, pamper wearing, rattle banging, snotty-nosed infants. The way I've described the above mentioned infant does not shake the parent because the parent loves that child and wants to help that child grow-up, potty train them, educate them, instill the love of God in them. The Christian parent realizes that God has a plan for their lives, a future, and a hope. (Jeremiah 29). Except for a medical problem, isn't it terrible to see a person still in diapers that is too old for diapers? Yet that is the condition of many people mentally, spiritually, and emotionally. Some are reading this and are thinking; well I've been a good parent to my child in all areas. I've done my job. I'm finished now. This reminds me of what a principal said at a teacher's staff meeting I was in… "The parents don't teach the kids manners anymore, right from wrong, yes sir, no sir, please and thank you. If the parents don't raise them right, we will. Treat them like you would treat your own." We have to be the rooted in love parent for whomever needs it.

WHAT HAPPENS WHEN YOU ARE ROOTED?

What happens?...Sandra's co-workers know she is a praying woman that gets results. Many times she will get prayer requests to pray for co-worker's family and friends that are sick or have a need. They will even stop by her desk on the way out to find out if she is praying any certain way concerning the weather, so they can make their plans accordingly. Having been in the same position for 20 years now at the University of Arkansas, people all over campus call her (and rely on her) for information that is not part of her job description.

What happens?...I'm not suppose to start discussions about God with kids at school. Over the years, kids have found out that I once was a pastor. So every once in a while kids ask me questions at lunch or recess about angels, heaven, hell, or some other topic that they are discussing among themselves.

What happens?...Out of the above discussions, students will come up to me privately and ask me to pray for them because they are going to have surgery, etc.

What happens?...In the last six years we have had seven students to die. When you are stable, these situations create opportunities to be a comfort to those around you.

What happens?...Teachers, staff and parents find out about you. They start showing up at your room before first bell or during your planning period and want to share a burden or a prayer request.

What happens?...Sandra does a thing called "Feed My Sheep"- she takes part of the groceries we buy and gives them to whom the Lord leads. Several times this has been a way to minister to co-workers. Relationships are built.

THIS WILL NEVER WORK

I know what you are thinking because I have thought the same thing. If I stay planted in this same job I'll never get ahead financially. As a teacher in the public school system (in a lower paying school district at that) I can relate. Let me share a couple of stories:

After attending my first year at L. S. U. and owing the large amount, at that time, of $800 for the year, I decided to drop out and learn how to be a bricklayer with my brother-in-law Nickie. I took out my room deposit and everything. Before the end of the summer, I had a great desire to go back to school. I had but one problem, no money. The high school English teacher showed up at my house and talked to my mom about a new federal program-B.E.O.G. (Basic Educational Opportunity Grant), she thought we would qualify. I did not even have her as a teacher, my brother and sister had. Never-the-less, I applied for the program. I received the total grant available; tuition, room, meals, books were all paid for the next 3 years! I believe God created this program in the legislature months before I had decided to go back. God had the United States Government add a program to fund my college! Not only was I blessed, but thousands of others over the years have been blessed.

I know, you are still thinking, "What about my pay raise?" Well, as I write, God is working with the Arkansas Legislature to change the formula on how money is given to the schools, basically- more money to the poorer rural school districts like Decatur. God is working on my pay raise! If He knows where I am and where Decatur, Arkansas is, He knows where you are and can catch up with you.

Something real interesting just happened. As I was typing the above paragraph I received a call from my wife telling me the Decatur middle school secretary's husband was calling the University of Arkansas trying to find a grad student to write grants for Decatur schools. My wife has nothing to do with grant writing. She was one of 20 or so transfers that the secretary's husband was put through. She told him who I was and that I had written some grants. (I have received a few small ones) So a few minutes later he calls and I talk with him a while. He then puts me on hold and connects me to a medical doctor in Decatur who is part of a local committee appointed by the superintendent to improve Decatur schools. He wants to know how we can attract more teachers and keep them. Are you kidding? I get to give him my spill on teacher salary differences between our district and the surrounding districts! As Leroy Thompson puts it "I'm not seeking after money, money is seeking after me!!!" Do you see how God is maneuvering people and circumstances? If I can believe it for me, I know you can believe it for you! Let me give you another story to show you how God can put people in your path.

I was in Clarksville, Arkansas attending a 4 day motivational conference that our elementary staff was attending.

There were 350 people attending this conference, ten males and the rest females. During registration they gave everyone a "Book Tote Bag". I called it a sissy bag; you know the kind you see elementary lady teachers carrying their stuff to school in. I met the lady that was in charge of the conference. Her name was Marie. She asked me how I thought we could get more men to attend these meetings. I jokingly told her that she had to get rid of the "sissy bags" for guys… give us a gym bag or a tackle box or maybe a tool box. I told her on a more serious note the way to get more men into teaching was to raise teacher salaries. That night I worked on a teacher's salary schedule that would attract and "keep the cream in teaching". The next day I saw Marie but she was talking to someone so I just walked by. When she saw me go by she said, in a loud comment to the man she was with, something about me and the sissy bags. So I turned around and handed her the salary schedule with the comments that she was an important woman that knows people in high places so it seemed and she was a go-getter type person so she surely could make the people in high places aware of the salary schedule. Finally when I get through my little speech to Marie about salary schedules, she backs up a step and puts her hand on her hips and says: "Do you know who this man is?" I look at him and say

"No I don't." Marie proceeds to introduce Senator John Brown from Siloam Springs, Arkansas to me. I turned back to Marie and said, "See I am a good judge of character, you do know people in high places! Give him a copy of the salary schedule and the directions on how to fund it!" God will bring the people across your path that you are supposed to meet! Don't worry about catching up with the money for the raises…

God has divine appointments waiting for you.

CRUISE-A-MATICS

This brings me to the idea that most people think they have to run around and "find the spout where the glory is coming out!" People hop from one church to the next in search of the "anointing". I have news for you. Your "spout" is over the ground where God desires for you to be planted. Go back and read that sentence a second time or a third time so it will soak in!

If you are planted anywhere else you will be like my dwarf trees- you will never be all that God has planned for you to become! You need to realize that God is over there watering and fertilizing the spot where you are SUPPOSE TO BE PLANTED. But you aren't there!

So will you just be there forever? Yes, plan on being planted where you are forever. Learn to be content wherever you find yourself. The Bible says obedience is better that sacrifice. Learn to hear God's voice. Obey what you hear God tell you to do. God will speak to you when it is time to move. When God and If God wants to transplant you, He will make it happen. "For promotion cometh neither from the east, nor from the west, nor from the south. But God is the judge: He putteth down one, and setteth up another." Psalms 75:6-7 (KJV). Remember God has you there for a reason. Find out what the reason is and fulfill His purpose for being there. The sooner you accomplish God's plan, the sooner the promotion will come. Hopefully you realize that all the while God is working some things out of or into your life. Let Him have the time to do a complete work in you.

Look at the story of David tending sheep. He wasn't sending out "King Resumes" to all the countries needing a king. He was planted and grew strong where he was. God knew his address. He knew how to get in touch with him.

As a young hungry Charismatic I would go to all the church services we had plus I would go hear special speakers anywhere within an eighty-mile radius. I would go hear Kenneth Copeland, Jesse Duplantis, Jerry Savelle, Kenneth Hagin, R. W. Shambach, Benny Hinn, etc. One time I rode my motorcycle 80 miles in the rain to hear R. W. Shambach. When I sat down after the song service I noticed a puddle of water where I had been standing! The temperature was in the 30's on the ride back that night-I was about frost bit. For several years now I have not taken such trips. Some may think I've become wise to not do something so foolish. Others may say I've lost my hungering for the Lord. Actually what has happened is that I realize that I do not have to run and be under another man's anointing. My relationship with the Lord has grown stronger. I've learned how to hear from God for myself. I've learned to get it direct from God. I still watch these guys on TV, read their books, and now ...listen to their podcasts! I'm still learning from them. It is just I'm learning to be more stable, grounded, rooted in love.

WHY BOTHER

You see God wants to put your life together not just so you will be some pretty little pot of flowers. No, God restores you and sends you out so that you can make a difference in this world. God wants to plant some of you in Washington, D. C. There are a few things that need your attention as a Christian rooted and grounded in God's love. Some of you He wants to plant in state and local government, school boards, and P.T.O. committees. Some God wants to plant in the business world. At the time of this writing Enron and other companies are starting to demonstrate what it is like when people not grounded in love are in control. God needs some people that are… come on now; don't make me name every job, profession, and place of work known to man! This is the MAJOR POINT I want to make in writing this book: God Needs You

Right Where You Are Now!!! So drop your landing gear, land, and start growing some roots. Stay open to His voice. He'll tell you if and when you need to move. One of the problems with the American society today is that we don't stay in one place long enough to make people relationships. That is why so many of our conversations with each other are so shallow. We talk about the weather, sports, food, etc. When is the last time someone opened up their heart and shared deep personal things with you? Do you even know someone you could do that with? So when was the last time this happened?

As a kid growing up (before 18 years old), I can think of at least 3 states we lived in, 7 different houses we lived in. After 18 years old till now (60 years old), it doesn't get any better- I've lived in 5 states, 17 different houses. As an adult I've had 14 jobs. The longest I've stayed at on a job before Decatur was 6 years. I've been at my current job in Decatur 20 years! This will be a record breaking year-hopefully in many ways.

ARE YOU PLANTED

Are you planted in your relationship to God? Do you know Jesus Christ as your Savior? Are you growing in this relationship? How can you tell? What differences are in your life now?

Are you planted in your family? Are you planted as a father, mother, son, daughter, husband or wife? Do you make a positive influence on their lives? How much time do you spend with them every day?

Are you planted at your job? Are you always looking for another job? Are you always complaining and part of the problem or are you part of the solution. Are you the "employee of the month" or are you the employee they want to get rid of this month?

Are you planted in your church? Do you know what your spiritual gifts are? Do you use your gifts and talents and skills in

God's kingdom? Do you support the church with your tithe? Would your pastor be shocked to see you in church two Sundays in a row? Would the pastor be more upset if you stayed in the church or if you left the church?

Take every area of your life and ask God to show you WHERE you are to be planted and HOW to do it. Then stay there till you hear his voice telling you to do something else. Not only will you be blessed but everyone around you will be blessed also.

IT'S TIME TO GROW UP... ROOTED AND GROUNDED IN LOVE!

This is the oak tree that was "flat-topped" due to the swarm of bees. It was cut down where I am pointing. Look at it NOW!

At age 62, I have retired from teaching. I taught 32 years, (21 years at Decatur). This book has taken almost 20 years to get written and published. Taking off six months, trying to decide what God wants me to do with the SECOND HALF of my life! Using this tree for inspiration, I would say the future is looking good!